Pamir

Also by Adrian Rogers and published by Ginninderra Press
The Sun Behind the Sun
Between Two Hemispheres
The Prisoner's Messenger
The Medicine Wheel
Music is a River of Life
A Way Less Travelled
Ecce Homo
Seasons, Situations and Symbols (Pocket Poets)
Flowers and Star Signs (Pocket Poets)
Human Nature & the Welfare State (Pocket Polemics)
Croagh Patrick (Pocket Places)
Port Victoria (Pocket Places)

Adrian Rogers

Pamir

To those who sailed the seas through long centuries of
endeavour, and especially that noble brotherhood,
the Cape Horners; we should honour the sacrifices they made,
and the lives given.

Pamir
ISBN 978 1 76109 276 3
Copyright © text Adrian Rogers 2022
Cover image: Ginninderra Press

First published 2022 by
Ginninderra Press
PO Box 3461 Port Adelaide 5015
www.ginninderrapress.com.au

Contents

Part 1: Looking Back
   From the Fireside in 2019 — 9
   Voices Heard From Beyond — 11

Part 2: In the Morning of My Days
   Building the Dream, 1905 — 15
   Launching Pamir — 16
   Night Watch at Sea — 17
   Seascape 1 — 19

Part 3: A Prize of War, A Middle-aged Challenger
   A Prize of War, 1918 — 23
   Changing Fortunes — 25
   Seascape 2 — 27
   Sail Against Steam – Realistically — 28
   A Prize of War – Reprise, 1943 — 29

Part 4: The Last Great Race, Port Victoria, 1949
   The Challenge Accepted – Loading — 33
   Out With the Tide — 35
   Seascape 3, Night Into Dawn — 36
   Southern Ocean Concerto – Race to the Horn — 37
   Rounding the Cape — 38
   The Northward Leg — 40
   Doldrums — 42
   The Homeward Run — 43

Part 5: Old Age and Apotheosis
   Changing Times — 47
   Seascape 4, A Task, Train the Young For Tomorrow — 49
   The Last Voyage – Buenos Aires, 1957 — 51
   Mid-Atlantic Apotheosis — 53

Epilogue
   Port Victoria, 2019   61

Part 1

Looking Back

From the Fireside in 2019

This winter night fire is an ember glowing sea red
flame-shot, spark flying, log falling
flaring
dying like an old life
damped down
scene changing

memories ranging, overcoming a haunting dread,
Pamir unforgotten calling
daring
the Cape Horn rollers, rife
with the unknown,
beyond predicting

like the things I knew, climbing a flexing mast
monkey-fashion, yard poised, hauling,
caring
not for storm or stress, knife
sharp winds flown
exchanging

terror for excitement, tossed against wave smash
salt tasting the wind's wild stress,
a rash
of laughter storm-seeing
more, the lash
of being

collapsed in a spark-jewelled log-jammed fire sea
wave flamed, dying down slowly
to flee
old hopes softly, lightly,
just to be
past time, free.

Voices Heard From Beyond

Port Victoria (2001)

They do not wait for nightfall
voices
wind/sand blown
down sloping streets towards the harbour
and beyond
continuing a sea call
across the sun sparked flash dance
of a deepwater channel
into the wind's drone
to and from Wardang Island's broken
low lying rock/black skirted shore
in a dancing day's delight
and seabird flight
under sun, cloud, wind and calm
restlessly inswept off land and sea
sharing with casual passers-by
fleeting memories

catching holiday makers
touching Port Victoria's tribute
to ships and men long gone
still circling
closing in
on that rose-garlanding memorial garden
listening,
rendering a lingering tribute
for those who made the fateful choice
bearing the wind's weight
responding to the sea's ongoing
siren singing
in a ringing time-placed sacredness
touching brass storytelling plaques,
whispering…
'You're not forgotten lads,
not forgotten.'

Part 2

In the Morning of My Days

Building the Dream, 1905

A sweated steel dream weighed
in the balances of hope
keel laid
facing the water strong sun glittering
beyond her birthing place,
a scheme of sinew challenging
the steam powered race
honouring indebtedness to sailing
across millennia
paid in full,

gulls wheeling across the estuary
wing-catching light
siren/call a Venus of the waves.

'Let rising and falling
maul and hammer
echo through the caves of creation
birthing you seaward unto us.'

'They that go down to the sea in ships'
the few remaining
facing glory and due peril
storm, calm, heat, cold,
bonded fellowship's laborious enduring
are swept
beyond time's slipway
into the cosmic ocean of infinity.

Launching Pamir

A northern summer's
silver/grey patched blue
is clarity of light, changeably
luminously
sun/shadow shifting
a mild North Sea breathing.

A bottle swung champagne flood
blossoms along her hull
shipwright's mauls lifting
and dropping
are a sea-sung, rhythmically
driving pulse edging her over
into wind and water
for the outfitting of a mystery,
masts stepped strong and deep
awakening her
to the beyond of all distances.

'They will remember in aftertime my kind,
let no breaker dismember my secrets,
none find or possess
what passes me under sun and cloud
so, raise your glasses
on my launching day
let time have her say
then the sea be my shroud.'

Night Watch at Sea

Eight bells,
and a change of watch…

no passing bell to unlatch
the night on a deck alive gently
beneath balanced feet,
Officer of the Watch
eyes tracing
under white/gold star struck
black horizon widening skies
a geometry of masts, yards
and standing rigging strung to abide
storm force calls of wind and tide

spread/light a sparked glitter's wide
infinitely floating moment,
a silver/pale half moon riding high
mirroring ocean's globe encircling
free running wildness
one thousand miles from land,
hushed, a night's passing
interpenetration
by the muted thud of widespread
softly billowing canvas
creak and slap of block, tackle,
and water hull-slipped rushing
under a sky overarching
muffles voices,
limits commands
full sail set and the wind steady…

eight bells,
and a change of watch.

Seascape 1

The Southern Ocean's
monumentally multi-choral
colour coded rhapsodic wildness
is a wilderness
surging, free soaring against
whoever dares surf
a fantastic hugeness
of long backed rollers
ink dark lightening unto sky blue
grey edging to steel
when the wind
though slacker in their depths
screams into bow lift
against sails overstressed
taking the whip
of skin stinging mane-flying scud
an ocean cavalry
charging like Mazeppa's Ride.

'Unto this last', a pride
of present day
round-the-world racers glide
on a light ray surfing
over the high wind's singing,
Rachmaninoff's Piano Concerto No. 2
on a yacht's radio
companioning to the edge of fear.

Summon then her ghost,
...long-destined *Pamir!*

Part 3

A Prize of War, A Middle-aged Challenger

A Prize of War, 1918

War is a marketplace,
'Winner takes All'
the outcome, a race
to exploit, a fall
from pre-eminence
and status, a place
without prominence.

A docked vessel –
herself no longer,
yards bare
a stranger to hope
is masterless awhile
as gulls wheel and swoop
geometrising interactive miracles
with river, sea and sky,

yet silently,
stronger than hope is she stirred
by sea-breathed echoes of command
crewed in a foreign tongue
calling for time-bound mariners
of an ancient craft,
but where are these?

Haters of steam
the capitalising god
and speed his prophet
few be they
but, by chance not quite none,
yet their mastery
no longer required…will
any sign to serve, inspired
against the dictates of commerce?

'Let who will buy her back
if she be so desired that love
trumps the price of war!'

Changing Fortunes

The sea is a store of changing fortunes
time adrift from its moorings
a relativity rift in eternity round
and beneath a glide-winging wanderer,
a womb
like the Galactic Centre above
and below
like sky dark/matching a cloud grey sea
a scanner
of white-shafting ice blinks
against
sea/sky merging volatility.

A horizon's emerging instability
disappears like old memories,
old skills passed down through histories
fickle in judgement
unforgiving as fate's
ponderously thunderous breakers
importuning, echoing shakers
pummelling the cliffs of South Georgia.

'Where, wandering sea-watcher
in this wildness, wet, and welter
is the mistress of sail?
In the helter-skelter rush to compete
with steam and oil
will you fail
or toil on to glory and grandeur
sentient within yourself, a voyager
escaping the time rift, forever?'

Seascape 2

The Morning Star drops
below night's lifting curtain
dawn's rim a whitening spread
blazes molten
a ship sails into the day
and a blaze flare leaps golden
into the sky.

Tall masts, spread canvas
and the Tabernacle's daylong
Pillar of Cloud
lift *Pamir* gliding into the dawn
a silent wonder
as the Morning Star fades into light
sea-flared
sun-flared silk-like white
wind ruffled
a restless, reposing merger
of water, light, ship
and white swooping
sun-circling
sun-calling birds,
these are the dance
the heralds of morning
on this day
when our destiny with them
is All, and One.

Sail Against Steam – Realistically

Time however was not bent back
nor capital retrained to reticence.

Racking speed's insistence
dislocated the craft of sail
seeding the end to a tale
of integrity disdained,
sending a beautiful sincerity
of mastery, the verity
of hard-edged austerity
into a past forgettable,
if deemed regrettable
by soothsaying insincerity.

'We shall not see their like again'
on slipways of time or eternity
trained by disciplining centuries
historically enduring,
so, throw the dice of destiny,
let *Pamir* and *Passat* prepare
their last great race
the final challenge
to a mechanistic god,
the race of a century…

yet will they always be sailing
the cosmic ocean of memory
beyond history.

A Prize of War – Reprise, 1943

War is a marketplace
'The winner takes all,'
a race to exploit a fall
from pre-eminence
a shifting prominence
a 'finders keepers' ace
replayed from an earlier time.

'There's life in the old girl yet...!'

An ominous bet
to a harsher rhyme
by wave-swept echoes
commanding
another strange crew
sailing under a foreign flag,
and the question is asked...

'Will age's ill-fitting shoe
delimit her scope,
her mastery no longer required?'

This catch-cry's taunting
whoever desires to buy her back
haunts the chance to recreate
her wake along the time-track
by one shake and throw of the dice
one last great race...

but let *Pamir* dictate the story.

Part 4

The Last Great Race, Port Victoria, 1949

The Challenge Accepted – Loading

A sharp bright edge of a day, salt taste,
sea pale gold fire spark-flashing a glittering

across the deepwater channel flittering
grey shadows hasting
flick foam flecking rock-jagged
Wardang Island,
a litter of calling white winging
wind-blown birds in a scatter-seeming ballet's
sun-wild streaming
cavort around the anchored racers.

In line astern two ships
'Unto this last'
drab-dark bare-yarded angularities
on light splattered water
are swarming work alive
loading fast
amid a storming bustle of lighters
wheat-bale packed
coming and going like water beetles

on a flare-dazzling light-hazed
floating clouded onshore morning,
mounded waiting bales shrinking
like eroding hills harvested
from labour trails blazed
across sun-hot lands scrub cleared
away beyond those anchored ships,
yet no pausing
until loading completed
hatches battened down
they wait to assert a sea-winged pride.

'Up anchor,
Pamir and Passat sail with the tide!'

Out With the Tide

Onshore watchers know
they will not see the like again,
the last page
of the last chapter turning
an almost burning
fiercely sparking brightness of a day
fussing puffing tugs
two ships in tow
the on-deck orderly tackle securing
men taking station to hoist sail.

No gale
sweeps Wardang Island's half concealed
fang-like razor teeth
and with danger clearing
the shoreline to port diminishes sunwards
a wide gulf to starboard opening out.

Light wave-top dances set to flout
forecast and rumour,
crews hoist sail wings
catching the wind
two ships press forward 'bone-in-teeth'
wakes widening creaming to perfection
gulls chorusing
sweeping swooping arcing
round mastheads windward straining
to the challenge.

Seascape 3, Night Into Dawn

Star fade,
an overarching sky greying easterly
leaches away the night
lamps dimming down
before dawn light's upward leaping,
no delaying our passage into
a whitening lightening fade-out into blue,
omens and sea dreams
will never drown our aspirations
tides flood or neap demean us now.

No storm yet disturbs
water rhythmic a slipped rushing
caressing hulls,
creaks, slaps, billows,
rigging and sails together
giving and taking any weather
eyes keen, hearts steady
when the sun's flare blazing
coursing the horizon's rim
skyward racing
is a bourgeoning Vedic hymn
as ride they up into swift/light spreading
the fanfare of morning
Poseidon's racers lifting
up/buoyed on cloudlike sweeps of sail
along the bird's way
the whale's way
the wandering watcher's way-going
in this our time, NOW.

Southern Ocean Concerto – Race to the Horn

The sea has jaws
under bleak un-limiting lead-grey skies
teeth foamed yellowing,
'Let the sea roar
and all the fullness thereof'
discord and threnody measuring
as bows dip into darkness
rising again
up long sloping wave backs
threat darkening to warship-grey
over Mappa Mundi's outermost world edge
'Where there be dragons'
bellowing at the abyssal drop
and two ships challenging the untamable.

Racing following seas
the ship chasers sweep decks
dislodging tackle unsecured
but 'who dares wins'
wide sails set
catching the Roaring Forties
reaching Cape Horn on a bet
vigilant in mastery
against the threat of broaching death,
a sharp Antarctic breath
from distant ice blinks
shadowed…
by that sea-ghost wandering
albatross wind-rider,
a wildness unfathomable released
in breakers thundering
against the Cape unleashed.

Rounding the Cape

Cape no farewell
in land fingers from the north
down-thrusting
no horn of plenty countering
the spell of ice
from Antarctica up-thrusting,
from the strait no knell
across a sea's narrowed
raging welter
no one in twenty reckoning
on hope, yet we prevailed despite
a thunder-echo-roaring
across a raging wilderness of water
no counting
on a past remembered
held fast in trust
over time beckoning
as yards and masts lurched wildly
under cloud torn skies

though hope did rise
beyond hope, with no bell tolling
for the lost
from slippery decks awash
none counting the cost
as we rode out a passage
course held between vice-like
ice/rock terrors pitching
rolling past the Cape
cold greying unto leeward until
beyond the unfathomable
uprising from triumph and disaster
we made the stuff of legend
as its master.

The Northward Leg

In the long return from cold
Cape Horn retreated
into memory morphing
to reminiscences in later years,
tall tales told round the fire
dreams, hopes, fears,
schemes anchored in unreality
yet the sum of our hopes
formed the tropes
of verse and song,
the Roaring Forties a memory
left in our long-scattered wake.

*'Our hearts might be strong
but the voyage will be long
and though storm and stress
cannot make of us less,
what will we be in a dead flat calm?'*

Lighter winds did encourage
the northward leg
Rio de la Plate beckon
Rio de Janeiro beg, but
'Faith is the substance of things hoped for'
reckoning on history
with maybe a modicum of hubris
keeping faith with destiny
and inaccessible mystery.

*'Will soporific doldrums be a balm
for the tough and seasoned such as we
or enervate rather than alarm
our resolving to be?'*

Doldrums

Between clockwise
counter/clockwise
current and wind flows
airless inertia's warm doldrums
flattened the sea
ships hulls mirroring
sails hanging motionless
lengthening shadows
cross stitching the surface
blood/fire sunsets flaming
unresponsive watery expanses,
expectations hanging dead
in breathless waiting
floating above darkness
unknowing
between fathomless
and uncharted
intuited fears of things hidden
from before the first dawning.

Half believing
we waited for what might
or might not rise
from depths beyond thought,
no ghost-white familiar
gliding now overhead,
until a mood swinging breeze
transcribed unreality's
irrationally haunting dread
into the old awakening.

The Homeward Run

Light breezes creased the sea's surface
out-breathing
sighing out of stillness
sails snapping
rigging creaking
wavelets soft slapping hulls

steel-sided echoes as gulls
out-called flurrying
balletic parabolic flight patterns
crossing soft surging airs
infiltrating
a not quite perfectly interfacing
'Calm Sea and a Prosperous Voyage'
but encouragement
for wind songs haze filtering
rough cleaned light veiled yellow
reflecting white,
wind spinning voices answering
the quick pulsed.

Steep Bay of Biscay waves repulsed
offset low grey clouds
mustering
above loud winds buffeting
yet not as in our Cape Horn
Southern Ocean Concerto
escaping dark oceanic jaws,
but sun/cloud interchanges
sailing to ends
beginnings
fusing home-callings

past Ushant Light, flashings
bright dart-like
off our starboard beam,
Bishop's Rock – away to port,
a four-point bearing
off the Lizard Head,
Falmouth, a coda's
rhyme-dashing finale
faith keeping with destiny
one last time.

Part 5

Old Age and Apotheosis

Changing Times

Age is not always kind to a ship of ghosts
dream silent
over-crossing waves of emptiness
to memory
not loosening the heart's bonds
de-activating challenges
denying an opportune finale.

'Au Claire de la Lune…'

diminishes, alas a bleak
attenuated beauty
as yards and masts
against moonlight's waning
speak softly into
a grey-tailed night's ending
awaiting the sun
eight bells and a change of watch.

'Come awake
to a sea-breathed
harbour breeze wafted,
calls by seabirds lofted,
the importunity
of those wishing you well.

*'Scheduling speed's spell
moniker of times changing
is devoid of empathy
bereft of rhyme,
though blooming yet
with a singular hope in time
beyond rusting
age-worn decay
stained rigging
salt incrustation.*

'Come awake, Old Girl, today.'

Seascape 4, A Task, Train the Young For Tomorrow

A movement incoming
across the Harbour Bar
and wind born a distant surf roar
is memory
scarring one trapped in a war
against idleness.

How far, can she fly
from numbing
rust eating inertia
the law of entropy
the score kept
by time-long sorrow?

Beyond a murmuring
wind lifted humming
to an echo surfing drumming
a gently insinuating swell rolling,
settling a long slow
rhythmical rise into falling
of glassily undulating
reflective surfaces
as seabirds flick wingtips
tagging the sun's
light/water dancing
sea spirits partnering
antiphonally distant singing…

*'Join our dancing, prancing,
encountering elementally, air,
fire, water, sea-spray, sunray,
magically raining light.
Our Mother – Star of the Sea
is saying…
"Train the youth of today,
make them men for tomorrow."'*

The Last Voyage – Buenos Aires, 1957

Star of the Sea unseen
presenting
day/night rising a Centre to Zenith
bright hope of a day
southern hemisphere winter light,
a crowded dockside
well-wishers jostling
the Blue Peter flying
on this day for youth like a ray
of sun thrown down at her feet
laughing, crying,
and a ship seaborne as if readied
for flying far out from time.

Rio de la Plate does beckon
tugs jostling,
Rio de Janeiro in time enticing
in vain
for the young outward bound
from winter's hard clarity
northeast into hoped for summers
'Unto this last'
petitioning
even as moorings off-cast
and tugs nudge her, side/slipping
into midstream.

*'O Mother, Mother
Star of the Sea
bless this voyage
old ship young crew.
Pray for the Wanderer
Pray for me
for white unfolding
wide-spreading wings free
for onlookers crowding shorelines
embracing Atlantic air, sea, light,
winged sun-dancing wanderers
far from land
shadow silent…'*

Mid-Atlantic Apotheosis

Is there life, in the old girl yet
or an ill-founded bet…a mockery?

Heedless youth
observe no shadow
uncaring, love's dreaming
seedless though desired
will disbar their maturing
from youth into age
foreboding
their *'Dies Irae'*,
yet they hear not the rage
dissonant, a sea-chant
or see in that light slant
the Sybil's warning.

On-flowing into air
light-dawning
bright waves scattering
a glitter white/gold sparking fantasia,
wind deck-lifting
up-stirs the sea
making wide-spreading sail wings
raise her as though into flying reflecting
old glories long past once gracing *Pamir*
fast passing away
'Unto this last',
pre-determining love's firing
the youth of their day
fast-onward a gliding destiny's decree
'inexorable as fate'
through day/night watch-keeping routines
early and late
under the wind song's
grey-white clouded piling horizons
greeting each dawn
sailing days-along,
on under night skies blooming with stars
golden eyed against black,
passing into winds
inexorably rising
making her leap
like an old steeplechaser
taking Beecher's Brook in her stride
one last time…

until abruptly thrust into
a storming chaotic unreasoning
jolting sprung rhythmic rhyme
off season…
a sail snapping attack
complacency shattering,

gale shredding clouds
shrouding
a sun no more seen,
steep/lifting a terror
of rollers dark-sided
freaking,
a seventh wave's battering
cargo shifting
the old ship listing to port
rigging tangling
sails tearing
Pamir unable to right herself
unresponsive
un-sharing…

'Save young hopes disintegrating
our aspiring selves cry out, souls
born of light…!'

but the deeps bell is tolling
for young and old toiling
through whip lashing
heart-stopped hours,
Atlantic's furious wailing
flailing coldly capriciously
savaging impedimenta
confusing would-be rescuers
ill-fating an outcome
when none can fly
nor other ships pass close by,
none interfering
with destiny's unravelling
for the alone-in-a-crowd ones
struggling with Death's howling
'Day of Wrath' tones,

yet I saw her
almost broken, but still
the acme of courage
trying stubbornly

desperately to rise
against oncoming overtopping
towering waves
spray scorning, whipping
her further listing hull…

*'Turning almost to windward
did you remember
the old glory days
of the Cape Horn run
long past long gone,
while you fought so hard
to bring your lads home?'*

*'Your hold on life not quite broken
though more than a token
seemed yet like youth's mockery
come back, taunting
a careless bet
on old age haunting
while you strove still to rise
overcoming
soul-daunting powers
a final strength summoning,
traditions of pride and service
for 'duty inexorable as fate'
defying the sea's irresistible challenge…'*

but even the strongest can be taken
overpowered
by storm-stressing age
masts, yards and rigging
dragging her further
ever further over
until she could no more rise
surrendering at the last
to the sea her mother
so longing to possess
that never would she let her go.

'Not for you the long sunset glow,
old age's adagio,
remembrance in tranquility,
but did you not say on your launching day…'

'They will remember in aftertime my kind,
let no breaker dismember my secrets,

none find or possess
what passes me under sun and cloud
so, raise your glasses
on my launching day
let time have her say
then the sea be my shroud!'

'We remember you, and your lads
unshadowed by age or fireside regrets,
perhaps, after all you did bring them home.'

Epilogue

Port Victoria, 2019

Roses bloom again
in the memorial garden,
a wind off the sea
and white/golden sun drops
dance on the waters of the Sound
running fast with the tide.

I gaze, eyes wide,
light does not harden the day
just stops thought in its tracks
while memory, off the mark
maybe, is still true
'Unto this last.'

Fishing lines are cast
from an empty anchorage
where once the lighters bustled
in their loading.
Sad, is it not…?

Slipping-by memories are my lot,
a wind off the sea,
a dying fire
ash soon to be cold,
yet the flame of desire
will always be
in faith kept, a story well told…

*'You're not forgotten lads,
not forgotten.'*

www.ingramcontent.com/pod-product-compliance
Lightning Source LLC
Chambersburg PA
CBHW062202100526
44589CB00014B/1913